EXTREME DINOSAURS

WORLD'S DUMBEST DINOSAURS

Rupert Matthews

Heinemann Library
Chicago, Illinois

www.capstonepub.com
Visit our website to find out
more information about
Heinemann-Raintree books.

To order:

☎ Phone 888-454-2279

💻 Visit www.capstonepub.com
to browse our catalog and order online.

© 2012 Heinemann Library
an imprint of Capstone Global Library, LLC
Chicago, Illinois

Edited by Rebecca Rissman and Laura Knowles
Designed by Richard Parker
Picture research by Mica Brancic
Originated by Capstone Global Library Ltd
Printed and bound in China by CTPS

15 14 13 12 11
10 9 8 7 6 5 4 3 2 1

Library of Congress Cataloging-in-Publication Data
Matthews, Rupert.
  World's dumbest dinosaurs / Rupert Matthews.
    p. cm.—(Extreme dinosaurs)
  Includes bibliographical references and index.
  ISBN 978-1-4109-4523-5 (hb)—ISBN 978-1-4109-4530-3
(pb) 1. Dinosaurs—Juvenile literature. I. Title.
  QE861.5.M3744 2012
  567.9—dc23   2011016081

Acknowledgments
We would like to thank the following for permission to
reproduce images: © Capstone Publishers pp. **4** (James Field),
5 (James Field), **7** (Steve Weston), **8** (Steve Weston), **8** (Steve
Weston), **9** (Steve Weston), **10** (Steve Weston), **11** (Steve
Weston), **12** (Steve Weston), **13** (James Field), **14** (Steve
Weston), **15** (Steve Weston), **16** (James Field), **17** (James Field),
18 (Steve Weston), **19** (Steve Weston), **21** (Steve Weston),
23 (James Field), **25** (James Field), **27** (James Field); © Miles
Kelly Publishing p. **24** (Chris Buzer); Shutterstock p. **29**
(© IPK Photography).

Background design features reproduced with permission of
Shutterstock/© Szefei/© Fedorov Oleksiy/© Oleg Golovnev/
© Nuttakit.

Cover image of a *Stegosaurus* reproduced with permission of ©
Capstone Publishers/Steve Weston.

We would like to thank Nathan Smith for his invaluable help
in the preparation of this book.

Contents

Dumb Dinosaurs? 4

Too Dumb to Fight 6

The Great Display 8

Inside the Brain 10

Armored Stupidity................................... 12

Bonehead 14

Fruit Eater 16

Sunbathing 18

A Second Brain....................................... 20

Puppy Brained 22

Brain Fever.. 24

Desert Walker 26

Dealing With Fossils 28

Glossary 30

Find Out More 31

Index 32

Some words are shown in bold, **like this**. You can find out what they mean by looking in the glossary.

Dumb Dinosaurs?

When **dinosaurs** were first discovered, many people thought they must have been the dumbest animals to ever walk the Earth. But today, scientists think that some dinosaurs might have been quite intelligent. Most dinosaurs were smarter than crocodiles!

Some dinosaurs had a huge body but a very small brain. They were probably dumber than other dinosaurs. However, we might never know how smart or dumb dinosaurs really were.

Did You Know?

Dinosaurs lived in a time known as the **Mesozoic Era.**

Too Dumb to Fight

Sauropods like *Apatosaurus* were huge, plant-eating **dinosaurs** with long necks and tails. *Apatosaurus* weighed about 30 tons. That is as heavy as six elephants!

Despite its huge body size, the brain of *Apatosaurus* was only the size of the brain of a modern cat. With a small brain and big body, *Apatosaurus* may have been really dumb.

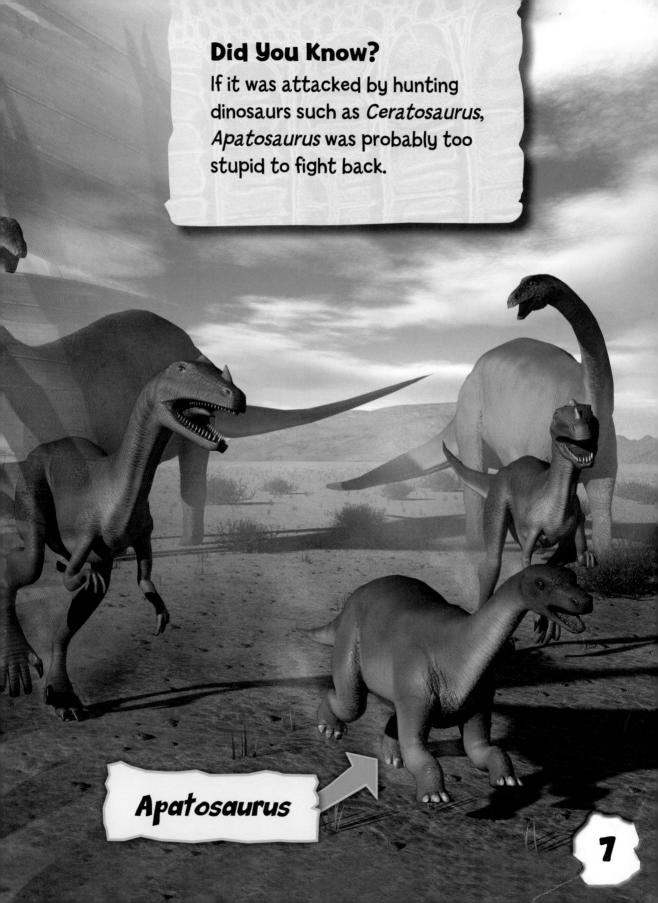

Did You Know?

If it was attacked by hunting dinosaurs such as *Ceratosaurus*, *Apatosaurus* was probably too stupid to fight back.

Apatosaurus

The Great Display

Argentinosaurus was around 121 feet long and weighed over 110 tons. That is about as heavy as 20 elephants. Its brain was no bigger than that of *Apatosaurus*. It must have used most of its brain power to control its big body! It probably had little brain power left over for thinking.

Did You Know?
The skeleton of *Argentinosaurus* on display at Fernbank Museum in Atlanta, Georgia, is the largest **dinosaur** on display anywhere in the world.

Inside the Brain

Scientists have found a **fossil** brain of *Tyrannosaurus*. The parts of the brain controlling smell and sight were large, but the thinking part was small. *Tyrannosaurus* probably found **prey** using sight and smell, and then attacked using brute force.

Tyrannosaurus

Armored Stupidity

The **ankylosaurian dinosaur** *Nodosaurus* had **armor** made of bone in bands over its back. Plates of bone armor protected its shoulders, neck, and head. If it was attacked, *Nodosaurus* would lie flat on the ground. This meant that its soft belly was protected. Maybe *Nodosaurus* was not smart enough to think of another way to escape!

Did You Know?
Struthiosaurus had spikes of bone as well as armor. It was no smarter than *Nodosaurus*.

Bonehead

The first **fossil** to be found of the **ankylosaurian** *Panoplosaurus* was a skull found in Alberta, Canada, in 1917. The skull was 2 feet long, but the brain inside was only about as big as a walnut. Almost all the skull was made up of bone.

Did You Know?

Only a few fossil parts of *Panoplosaurus* have been found, so scientists view it in different ways. The pictures show two versions of *Panoplosaurus*.

Fruit Eater

Pawpawsaurus was an **ankylosaurian** that lived in Texas. Its name means "Pawpaw Lizard." Scientists gave it this name because they think it ate soft fruits like pawpaws. *Pawpawsaurus* probably wandered slowly around eating fruits and did not need to think much. It probably had spikes on its shoulders and **armor** all over its back and tail.

Pawpawsaurus

Sunbathing

Stegosaurid dinosaurs like *Hesperosaurus* or *Lexovisaurus* had large plates and spikes growing from their backs. Some scientists think these growths protected the stegosaurids from attack. Other scientists think the plates were used to soak up warmth from the Sun. Warm blood means brains can work faster.

Hesperosaurus sunbathing

Lexovisaurus being attacked by two *Megalosaurus* hunters

19

A Second Brain

Stegosaurus was a plant-eating **dinosaur**. Inside its hips was a large space. This space may have held a type of second brain. This would allow the dinosaur to move quickly if it was attacked. However, some scientists think the space was filled by other body **organs**. So the *Stegosaurus* may have been quite dumb after all.

Puppy Brained

Kentrosaurus could grow to almost 15 feet long, about the length of a car. Its brain was only about the size of a puppy's brain.

Kentrosaurus might have been unable to think of clever ways to defend itself. If it was attacked, *Kentrosaurus* could face away from its enemy and wave its spiked tail around.

Kentrosaurus

Did You Know?

Huayangosaurus was the smallest known **stegosaurid**. Its brain was about as big as an apple.

Brain Fever

The tallest **dinosaur** was probably the **sauropod** *Brachiosaurus,* which lived in North America about 150 million years ago. It was almost 35 feet tall—taller than most houses. Its brain was so small you could hold it in one hand.

Brachiosaurus

Desert Walker

Fossils of *Plateosaurus* have been found in rocks that may have since formed into desert. *Plateosaurus* may have walked from one feeding ground to the next.

Plateosaurus fossils have been found in what was mud. Perhaps the **dinosaur** was so stupid that it got stuck in mud and could not get out again!

Plateosaurus

27

Dealing With Fossils

Once scientists have found a **dinosaur fossil**, they need to **excavate** it. First the soil and rock on top of the fossil is removed. Next the fossil is removed from the rock in which it has been preserved. The rock may be chipped away with a **chisel**, scratched off with a metal prong (fork), or **dissolved** with acid. The fossil is then wrapped in bubble wrap or cotton to be taken to a museum for study.

Glossary

ankylosaurians family of armored, plant-eating dinosaurs that lived between 160 and 65 million years ago

armor outer shell or bone on some dinosaurs that protected their bodies

chisel metal tool with a sharp end

dinosaur group of animals that lived on land millions of years ago during the Mesozoic Era

dissolve melt into a liquid

excavate dig something out of the ground

fossil part of a plant or animal that has been buried in rocks for millions of years

Mesozoic Era part of Earth's history that is sometimes called the "Age of Dinosaurs." It is divided into three periods: Triassic, Jurassic, and Cretaceous.

organs parts of the body such as the heart and lungs

prey animal that is eaten by another animal

sauropod family of plant-eating dinosaurs that had long necks and long tails. The largest dinosaurs of all were sauropods.

stegosaurid group of plant-eating dinosaurs that had spikes or plates of bone sticking out of their backs and tails

Find Out More

Books

Bingham, Caroline. *Dinosaur Encyclopedia.* New York: Dorling Kindersley, 2009.

Lessem, Don. *The Ultimate Dinopedia.* Washington, DC: National Geographic Children's Books, 2010.

Markarian, Margie. *Who Cleans Dinosaur Bones?* Chicago: Heinemann-Raintree, 2010.

Matthews, Rupert. *Ripley Twists: Dinosaurs.* Orlando, FL: Ripley Publishing, 2010.

Websites

science.nationalgeographic.com/science/prehistoric-world.html
Learn more about dinosaurs and other facts about the prehistoric world at this National Geographic Website.

www.ucmp.berkeley.edu/
Learn more about fossils, prehistoric times, and paleontology at this Website of the University of California Museum of Paleontology.

www.nhm.ac.uk/kids-only/dinosaurs
The Natural History Museum is located in London, England. Its Website has a lot of information about dinosaurs, including facts, quizzes, and games.

www.kidsdinos.com/
Play dinosaur games and read about dinosaurs on this Website.

Index

ankylosaurians 12–17
Apatosaurus 6–7, 8
Argentinosaurus 8–9
armor 12, 13, 16, 18

bone plates 12, 18
Brachiosaurus 24–25
brains 4, 6, 8, 10, 14, 18, 20,
   22, 23, 24

Canada 14
Ceratosaurus 7

excavate 28

fossils 10, 14, 15, 26, 28

Hesperosaurus 18
Huayangosaurus 23
hunters 7, 10, 19

Kentrosaurus 22

length 8, 22
Lexovisaurus 18, 19

Megalosaurus 19
Mesozoic Era 5

Nodosaurus 12

Panoplosaurus 14–15
Pawpawsaurus 16–17
plant eaters 6, 16, 20
Plateosaurus 26–27
prey 10

sauropods 6–7, 24–25
sight 10
skeletons 9
skulls 14
smell, sense of 10
spikes 13, 16, 18, 22
stegosaurids 18–19, 23
Stegosaurus 20–21
Struthiosaurus 13
sunbathing 18

Tyrannosaurus 10–11

warm blood 18
weight 6, 8